# Turbulence

**Thuy On**

Thuy On is an arts and literary journalist and critic who has written for a range of publications including *The Australian*, *The Age/SMH*, *The Saturday Paper*, *ArtsHub*, and *Books + Publishing*. She's also the books editor of *The Big Issue*.

**Other titles in the UWAP Poetry series (established 2016)**

*Our Lady of the Fence Post* J. H. Crone
*Border Security* Bruce Dawe
*Melbourne Journal* Alan Loney
*Star Struck* David McCooey
*Dark Convicts* Judy Johnson
*Rallying* Quinn Eades
*Flute of Milk* Susan Fealy
*A Personal History of Vision* Luke Fischer
*Snake Like Charms* Amanda Joy
*Charlie Twirl* Alan Gould
*Afloat in Light* David Adès
*Communists Like Us* John Falzon
*Hush* Dominique Hecq
*Preparations for Departure* Nathanael O'Reilly
*The Tiny Museums* Carolyn Abbs
*Chromatic* Paul Munden
*The Criminal Re-Register* Ross Gibson
*Fingertip of the Tongue* Sarah Rice
*Fume* Phillip Hall
*The Flaw in the Pattern* Rachael Mead
*The Sky Runs Right Through Us* Reneé Pettitt-Schipp
*Walking with Camels* Leni Shilton
*Wildlife of Berlin* Philip Neilsen
*Aboriginal Country* Lisa Bellear
*Moonlight on Oleander* Paul Hetherington
*Broken Ground* Steve Armstrong
*Satan Repentant* Michael Aiken
*Open Door* John Kinsella
*Poor Man's Coat* Christopher (Kit) Kelen
*Stone Mother Tongue* Annamaria Weldon
*Legacy* Julie Watts
*Keeper of the Ritual* Shey Marque
*The short story of you and I* Richard James Allen
*Autobiochemistry* Tricia Dearborn
*Vishvarūpa* Michelle Cahill
*The little book of sunlight and maggots* Michael Aiken
*Bone Ink* Rico Craig
*Malcolm: a story in verse* Leni Shilton
*The Other Flesh* Robbie Coburn
*ReDACT* Ross Gibson
*Infernal Topographies* Graeme Miles
*boots* Nadia Rhook
*Case Notes* David Stavanger
*A History Of What I'll Become* Jill Jones
*Self ie* Alice Savona

# Thuy On
# Turbulence

First published in 2020 by
UWA Publishing
Crawley, Western Australia 6009
www.uwap.uwa.edu.au

UWAP is an imprint of UWA Publishing,
a division of The University of Western Australia.

ISBN: 978-1-76080-125-0

A catalogue record for this
book is available from the
National Library of Australia

Designed by Becky Chilcott, Chil3
Typeset in Lyon Text by Lasertype
Printed by McPherson's Printing Group

Dedicated to the younger me:
you'll weather the turbulence.

# Contents

## Surface

Let others wax mauve
about dandelions and baby's breath
bracing cool breezes
that brush off regret
these winsome odes to blades of grass
dewy mists and sheaves of corn

let others decry the cut and thrust
of a world riven
and split by codes
fly-flecked in drying blood
these Faustian pacts
my words care not for such

but rather burrow
beneath this landscape
excavate the found
gem or stone
and surface in air
to breathe.

# Wreckage

## Double bind

I took it off months ago
a hand now stripped bare
a tongue worrying
a toothless gap
the loss niggling
a psychic reminder
until what was left

was only skin
a worm in the sun
the pale band of absence
now tanned over
even you can't tell
what was there
yes

flip the hand over
see the lifelines
this promise
that heartsore
the collision of movement
a damning of past
(im)perfect.

## Crossfire

Imagine
the ecstasy of plates
crashing down

hard-edged snowflakes
this pure assault
a subcutaneous hit

viscosity pooled
in ever widening arcs
imagine

half-skittered deer
uncamouflaged
bullseyed

a lolling tongue
a misted red.

## Pestle

We were the sun
dipping low
long past its zenith

we were marked
scratching at calluses
leached of life

me depleted
pestled into powder
away from you

the ground
loosely packed
air I can taste

away from you
we were the sun
the process has begun.

## Sisyphus

This life
roughly patched over
tender skin shows
a bruise without fade

This life
vinegar splashes
into freshwater
an oil slick to sink

This life
Sisyphean climbs
falter in valleys
a drop to the knees.

# Haemorrhage

A necklace of
bloody beads
is trailing behind me
hitting the pavement
deep blossoming rubies

this heart-gape
fist-shape
trickle a leak
I look down in surprise
O-mouthed there

could be so much
seepage still
I thought plasma cells
and these eye salts
were exhausted

beyond my shoulder
these stains they follow
and every step
a rhythmic beat
such metallic puddles.

# Mosaic

In this taxonomy
of laddered pain
eyes need to be drawn
to the jar that holds the tulip

a firebird bathing in ashes
splinters of glass
crystallised into prisms
a tabula rasa

no echo no hum
a muffle of white noise
breathing in and out
in and out

a hushing of the mind
a gilt-edged clarity
to look ahead
mosaic the rear-view mirror.

## Lodestar: To Ava

Your mother
is an in-betweener
in transitional mode
from what is
to what will be
over the shoulder glance:
spoiled
a throat-scorching landscape
for the love of you
I tried to make the triangle prevail
until enough
I could prop no more
a collapse of this formation of sticks
stones that did hurt
a soul in unfashionable black

shield your eyes darling girl
I don't know
what will become of us
a looking forward
a dazzle
for this tiny binary unit
is all I can write for
those who spark
then fade
will make their presence felt
but you
you are the lodestar

to light me out
a reminder
of a life to be kissed.

# Holy Trinity

It's Sunday
a nuclear unit spills out
baked bread and all that is wholesome
froth on pink-button noses
woollens tight on acorn heads
those pitter-pats on backs
father mother child

at a table for one
my coffee spoon clatters
grains of sugar over yesterday's news
the child startles

eyes like saucers
she breaks out
from the ambit of care

and comes to me
licks a finger sweetens the tip
with fallen crystals

a sudden violence
my chair kicked back
I cross the street
there's a bite to the air.

# Tense: continuous present

I'm in the wrong book
and flung against the wall
words dribble down:
conjunctions split
nouns become con
exclamation points once sentinel
lie on their backs
transformed into
dashes and full stops.

# February 14

Paired up
a Noah's Ark of smugness
these bipeds
and their velvety refuge
I want to rose prick fingers
on this blush-coloured
rictus grin of a day

me? a swamp croak of frogs
awaiting kisses
a sky of fallen stars
to trip over
a heart
Houdini-trapped
without a key.

# Centrifugal forces

I sink in the bath
my fingers soft prunes
bubbles trembly afloat
dissolve into tears
head back neck open
bare-faced vacant
at cracks in the ceiling
the choices made
in this hourglass stalled
a house not my own

a suitcase engorged
the sweet-smelling water
as I lie here
a centrifugal force
I close my eyes
the white tiles
a trellis of green leaves
framing the room
breathing quietly
for me.

## Kintsugi

What hope
to behold
such beauty in the broken
the lacquer that fills edges
a delicate repair

such precious scars
these fractures restored
a joinery visible
silvered with hands
mindful

of what it takes
to be held to the light
for hairline cracks
a caressing wipe over
the whole.

# A new vocabulary

Tectonic plates
sliding into
or breaking apart
a scrabbling for purchase
a gasping of lungs

constant 3 am
eyeballs wired
a time set aside for
neural conjugation
a rubric for living

lone (ly)
free/bore (dom)
happy (less/ness)
(n) ever more
depending on barometer.

## Perspective

Can you frame yourself in 3rd-person
outside this life, not of your choosing?
a soundtrack

but at a remove
theatrics muted, outlines fuzzy
tiny cymbals and violins

just a slice of the drama
on reveal
like a fingernail clipping of the moon.

# Shogyo mujo

Transience as a gift
these moments parcelled
on a conveyor belt
to final breath

discrete units to linger
or suffer over
watch them pass by
haphazard and unguessing

you can't, you don't know
what days carry within
a waiting, a hoping
for opening.

# Vantage

Maybe
the grass is greener over there
because it was watered
leaving these browning spearmint blades
to furl into themselves

maybe
what faltered in this patch of square
was your black thumb's work
this creep of corner sun
a dying reach for rest

maybe
beyond these tinted windows
a cotton-woolled
crayon blue vista
birdsong carried by wind.

# Whirling dervish

To colour inside the lines
I have to
*coffee poetry cupcakes sex*
to recall the muscle memory

of non-calamity
I have to
*obviate mitigate cultivate*
to spin the wheel

I have to
*land pointer thrust*
*diametrically opposite*
to where it was stuck.

## Undergrowth

If you saw me open
these concentric rings
speak of light gathering
a push through a break

through to that shard
of blue blankness over
the littering copse
of the fallen and dead

take heed with every tread
that bark around smoothness
would bleed your fingers
time has not been too kind

go slow go gentle
the undergrowth will mark
your presence in tiny shoots
freshly dewed and lifting.

# Sunflower

Reams of dead trees
deadlines for other peoples' words
sunk under the pressure
of domestic detritus
I am unread and shelved
a paperweight
between seasons
a cobwebby head needing to shake
for the new year beckons
this chance to flatten the path behind
roll it up and throw it hard
watch in awe the motes falling down
blinding the dusty ways

it's over
a clean lingua franca
lessons and spite
swallowed up spat out
the translation not lost
but tooled in stone
I know now what to do
as a sunflower
fed from blood in loamy soil
minerals of salty tears
through showerbursts and thunder
I toss my halo
gold.

# Chimera

## Curtains drawn

A room for rent
indifferently sleek

curtains drawn
traffic on mute

I pace for you
not quite stranger

not quite known
steps to traverse

this line to next
touch hunger sated

mind now stilled
the low lamp glows

illuminating sheets
whipped egg whites

our angles our
mounds

green tea bath
sloughing off world

cleansed we sway
to the drag of sleep

your midnight kiss
embrace.

# Art

I want you to draw me
frame me
capture me in chiaroscuro
like the mirror that pins us

so artfully as we move
the tableau now frozen
then languid
limbs draped and decorous

your eye my eye
a gaze clean and unbroken
look: our reflection
you prone me rearing above

a soft attack
I take you in.

# Red

Red is the dress
fire-engine sheen
Red is the siren call
come come closer
Red is the lip stain
bloodshot eyes
at the pencil-thin line
between dusk and dark
the curve of my heart
the hum of your pulse
Red is the tissue
the drum of hunger
the beat of now
Red is the dress
kicked to the dust
as I come up for more.

## Tattoo

I want to trace it on your wrist
a memento you confessed
a keeping of faith
I want to lick the sweat
off your brow

I want to hide your glasses
so you see in silhouette
and have to feel
to find me
an arm's reach away

I want to unzip your mouth
green light your eyes
to go go go
I want to peel off that rock star skin
expose your trembling core
in ink.

# Oasis

I spy
this crumpled shirt
its blueness
an oasis
in the white of sheets
the buttons I unpicked
through touch alone
as mouth on mouth
and eyelids closed
I came

I spy
this fine negligee
a flimsy sheathe
discarded so fast
you knew what it held
you felt through the wrapping
a ball of black
a scrap of deliverance
offered to you
as I came.

## Black and gold

Golden as your name?
I think much darker
a dull burnished noir
streaks through your veins
of Lynchian punk flicks
scarred skins
fright masks
champion that you are
of femmes fatales
from hybrid races
with hard guitar riffs
ripping
the heavy air

golden as your name?
you are
of slick stiff hair
crow-gloss
a fine-featured boss
culture vulture
picking off bones
a heavy-booted rebel
with causes to burn

yet sweet as licked candy
timorous as spun floss
this speck of gold
beneath black.

# Muse

Barely do I know you
and yet you cause
words to spill out
random body contact
a cut to the system
and I bleed
profusely
so many letters
scarlet and ragged
a contusion
of emotions
once contained
now an exhalation
a relief
thought bubbles bursting
float to the air
for you to catch.

## Away

I wonder what flavours
assail you
in the dripping moisture there
the lush green
splicing through towers
that rip the sky into ribbons
I see you

    shimmer through waves
of coloured smog
sucking on fleshy fruits
in snarling traffic
ice slipping down your throat
in fluorescent malls
this blood sub-tropic home

    of forbears
a taut string that pulls and pulls
just know I am thinking of you
on nights mosquito warm
befuddled by time zones
I wonder: are you awake?
or sleeplessly restless

like me
this soupy heat
that clings tight around your body
these feverish dreams
that pique my longing
this slow clock watch
that awaits your return.

## Still life

How does it feel
to see yourself:
face, body, actions
stolen
subject turned object
abstract into concrete
wisp of emotions butterfly-netted
a flash Polaroid in words
where careless gestures
weighted with meaning
transmute into art
the beholder and the muse

a reciprocity
of zen and movement
just you and me
this alchemy
an inexact science
a still life contoured
in sharp pointed lines
that will survive us both
when dust is dust
these scraps
that bore witness
to youth
and heat
and heedlessness.

## 2D to 3D

I ask for a picture
memory a grey fade
the precise line of your lips
slope of bicep and belly

needing to be inked afresh
so brow and nose and mouth
may cohere in space
these pixels: a witness

piecemeal now whole
a facsimile but true
till I can trace
where eye has lingered

mirror you
heart to heart
heat for heat
touch upon touch upon touch.

# Traffic lights

In dimmed vision
we sit palm in palm
denouement already known
to me: I can risk it
close my eyes

ride on the current
softly delicious
your fingers edging my thigh
your profile angled to screen
attentive and still

my thoughts charging
already outside
breezing along the sultry air
the cityscape a neon nightflight
generous glittering

in summer bounty
and later at the lights
I kiss you
a stop then an amber
as hesitancy fights with want

tension pushes me
to test the shyness within
public
private
desire

display
a bird fluttering
one to the other
and then a green
and go.

## Fantasy story

So the Manga boy and the dark angel
meet again
their graphic novel to be played out
this time
in a sweetened womb

tealight candles
with tiny tongues
lap in anticipation
cloying scents entrapped
between walls

let's read this fantasy
to bolt the gate
against the glaring worrisome
outside
my black wings

in repose
flattened
to the curve of my back
their webbed lace
a delicate drape over shoulders

cosy soporific
on ruffled light sheets
I wait for foot treads
to rouse
and arouse.

# Absentia

How mighty really
is this pen?

a sleight of hand
to collapse together

the Joker and the King
a lover in absentia

yes I can see you
bare-chested supine

half-lit eyes on the moving screen
your dark hair awry

when we tumbled
slickly neat again

soft laughter escaping
the inanities of sitcoms

me in the corner
up standing

sweeping the panorama
already a camera

the lamps a dull witness
clothes in hills on the floor

this room this date
cut sharply in time

to be mildewed into nostalgia
but now for now

half-tunelessly to 80s pop
I still hear you sing.

# Shapeshifter

In three months' time
what shape will you take?
what configuration of form

will replace heart and mind
when cleansed of the soot
gathering beneath?

to banish your demons
and whitewash your soul
a body replenished

a garden watered
weeds burnt to dust
I hope to be there

when you come up to the light
a mantra on your lips
clear-eyed and blinking.

## Cameo

In this game of chance
the dynamic chaos
that whirlwinded us both
whimpers and waits
for pattern and tidy

the idea was to be
interwoven into narrative
separate skeins
gently plait bound
singular becoming plural

but your cameo sightings
make us a poor play
half-formed ghostings
creaking on floorboards.

# Display

You should be
calibrated and tagged
like those glorified artworks
three storeys of pleasing and provoking
a space on those walls
should have your name affixed
because I want to gaze

with thirsty eyes
take you in quick sips
to ward against future drought
your exact measure of leg
unruly flop of fringe
slope of shoulder to arm
a statue fine and crude
a false idol

this meta-narrative
as you contemplate paintings
a loop unbroken
your transfixion
my absorption
your interest elsewhere
mine stops
in a pulse.

# The shape of you

The universe is toying with me
because shortly before seeing the movie
the ending of which was a poem
about seeing the shape of you everywhere
I saw your doppelgänger

to blunt the rudeness
I stared through tinted lenses
at this simulacrum
a familiar composite
of cheekbones and helmeted hair

your uncanny twin
and in between station stops
I wallowed in
an alternative magic
a crack in time

where he whom
I'm torn over
looks over to me
a version, a kin
but not you

free and open
then a shuddering halt
and we disembark
he weaves through the crowd
disappears like a phantom

and I
I blink and shrug
and go to meet you
to watch a green-blue melodrama
a watery dream

shot through with iridescence
where fairytale
floats into consciousness
and for just a few moments
I believe.

## Astor

I drove in peak dust
an hour of bumper vibrations

to see a double feature
but you were the opening

the end credits
and everything in between

saved from a premature death
the grand Astor beckoned

defiant and sprightly
the come-hither brass and velvet

the parting of those
golden curtains

kitsch action glam horror
unravelling in technicolour

unspooling you in their glory
yet you couldn't see

an osmosis of affection
cynicism held in check

a particle of light
as I brightened in the gloom.

# Lust to dust

Just friendship
is all I can offer
you say
and this qualifier
makes all the difference
for me:
a bouquet denuded of buds
the core
petrified in ice
eyes blinkered
hands gloved
from touch
I wish I could drink
a truth serum
but heart-sobered
strait-jacketed
I self-edit
just.

## See-saw

If I could write you out of my system
I would
siphon every last drop away
drain the bloodstream
of residual traces
flatten memory
and sandpaper flesh
where skin impressed
upon skin
on your audio track
I would press delete

but there's no antidote
just time's slow crawl
and this see-saw need
to recall
months of fitful joy
when in tune
a pas de deux
we gleamed in a bubble
lightweight
untouched
from the creases of the world.

# Tu me manques

In both languages
I miss you and
you are missing
from me
I am a glass
an x-ray
a stuttering
out of order
and denial is the pea
beneath mattresses
stacked ceiling high
the keen nub
tearing a hole through
sleep.

# Skull space

To wean
means time and distance
but you still rattle

in this skull space of mine
a marble ricocheting
between bone walls

how can I replace you?
mortal now symbol
inviolate and gleaming

these wasteland of suitors
and the pang in my chest
continues to thrum

brilliant and distracting
I blend into violet
and fall.

## Black spots

Yes I know
I put a crown on you

it sits askew
you are young

and the need to scorch
your path

the garments
that require trying on

before disrobing
are reminders why

the use-by date of us
was half-past yesterday.

## Numbers and words

Five months since
you were bidden
sans strings

a hotel plush in town
a birthday present for myself
a receiving and a giving

you were late
I paced barefoot
the sky deepened

in the apricot dawn
the words came
flutters of paper

poems like confetti
a ticker-tape parade
shower over you

free from their creator
a force field of their own
to keepsake or bonfire.

# Animus

This animus
between what you feel
and what you know

this cordon that drags one
blinds the other
for force of struggle

rope burns
sleep walks
into arms unable to bear

my weight
a studied deafness
to the meaning of casual

already what we had
dissolves frame by frame
a few more reels

and the credits will run
a scrim to be draped over
you and me

sheeted furniture
in an abandoned recess
and now and then

under the covers
the creaky joints
that linked us.

# Despondentrage

There really should be
a German term
for sad and mad
a portmanteau for this
unblessed union
a balance of
*despondentrage*

these last months
the sundial of my attention
shifted and slanted
never in shade for long
you were irradiated
a rose-gold lustre
now this void

from pursuit to retreat
where hurt goes to hide
and what was given is shut away
a silence as powerful
as any words
that were cupped in hand
over you.

## FIN

I'm turning the last page
it was supposed to be a short story
but unwilling for it to end
I kept tacking on chapters
footnotes where emotions cross-refer
erased    stet    highlighted
blanked out

there were mistakes throughout:
false notes uneven tone
an unreliable protagonist
desperate for an editor's pen
but I wrote as a lover
forgiving and forsaking
ink-splat

the story does not fly
dirt crusted and wormy
it will sit in a bottom drawer
among the strings of memory
borne of a hundred paper cuts
this love note that was
but no longer is.

# Fish

# Repair

There is an air-releasing valve
that for this ventricular repair
a master craftsman must attend
to stitch and staunch the flow

not these bumbling knaves
these one-night acrobatics
a row of single players
requiring a double act.

# Caveat emptor

Whoever reaches out
and stickers
a small red dot
an intent to claim
a plea, please
be gentle

so much invisible stitching
around these scarlet lips
so much dull
around these eyes
vertebrae
in load-bearing crumple

there is a need for
a kindness to buff
such coarsened patches
to right
what's ill-aligned
a ministering of twinset

patience and plaster
and in return
for this investment?
a blue-flamed passion
for the one who can
tender such sparks.

# Rom coms ruin it for everyone

In shopping aisles
banana is innuendo
in pavement stumbles
Mr Floppy Fringe comes a-dashing
while Little Miss Good Times
sashays behind tweed
and owlish specs

let's wait for:
boy meets girl
histrionic swells
riverbed of tears
lines criss-crossed
doubled up backed away
missteps

(an age later)

Venn diagram overlap
like and like meet halfway
a head knock heart pound body roll
after: a bench sit
skyline view
a shopping trolley where innuendo
is a peach.

## Playthings

Like hard-boiled lollies
bright buttony shine

the aftertaste of sweet and sweat
I will pick them up

these random pebbles
and skim the surface of water.

# Swipe left

Go scratch your boy band vinyl
your bae-babe-baby
bind up your geisha doll fetish
tight in a foot-sized box

an Oriental tease?
no not me
Marvel comics?
not a book

*if you wanna be my lover*
hey girl u r hot!
not my language
just watch me
ssswi-swipe left.

# Online dating in 5 haikus

Hello how are you?
inbox of generic tease
    sigh    ignore    delete

Ghosting & breadcrumbing
here now but gone tomorrow
    language of defeat

RSI thumb swipes
to fish bikes gyms naked gloss
    all players elite

Just one unicorn
among these unseemly beasts?
    a mythical treat

Dates of coffee dregs
resigned to cat companion
    heart hibernates, peace.

# Freelancer

No resting place
for these tired bones
a shift every few weeks:
these transferable parts

of players and their offers
to wrap a veil around the
clamour and hurtful light
to ignore for a beat

life's urgent pressing face
against the glass so smudged
crisscrossed with patterns of palms
stretched out and demanding in.

# Tinder-burnt, Bumble-fumble and Ok-stupid

Where's my partner in crime? I'm from the school of hard knocks
the university of life here for a good time not a long time just seeing
what the fuss is about I have no baggage and neither should you I'm
easy-going fluent in sarcasm & banter I like Netflix and chill and bars
and whisky but if you don't look like your pics your buying me drinks
until you do but hey no drama queens okay just here for fun y'know
will ruin your lipstick not your mascara standing 6 feet in heels
taller than you (cos apparently that matters) my kids are my world
but travel is the best Look at me in boardies against Machu Picchu
In sunnies with a dying trout In a rented tux crossed-armed with a
bunch of lads at me mate's wedding In a Bintang singlet at the beach
Squatting next to a dopey tiger At the footy with a gurnsey and scarf
Doing crossfit with no top at all (so I can show off the tatts)! Check
out my wheels! How about a bathroom selfie under 1000-watt light?
No? Something arty then half an eyebrow a close up of the kisser? I'm
after something casual ONS NSA GSOH ethical non-monogamous
poly oh yes must like dogs! No princesses! just here for fun I've done
a couple of salsa classes good at massages too no that's not my kid
and that's my sister don't be shy are you DTF? You up? oh I can't be
fucked writing 20 words here are some emojis don't bloody use those
Snapchat filters not here to follow you on Insta don't wanna penpal!
Want to know more? just ask Does anyone ever talk here?

## *Online Dating for Dummies*

Be the chased not the chaser
flatten down those
quivering endings
those exposed nerves
heightened to feel
such elation
at a wisp of connecting
thoughts and the charge
of communing skin electrics
those matches
flicks of convenience

a game of ego-stroked numbers
and disposability
write your own rules
1. caution over heartspill
2. truth is a sandblaster
3. roll roll the dice again

remember
algorithms don't compute
you are not a fraction
but a prime number
factor of one and itself.

# Seismograph

You are
so close you can slice me open
those loops of viscera
like liquid night

what you can't see:
churning wants
a pool of trepidation
a reflex to recoil

radii as counterbalance
of give and take
I give you me
take your reading now.

## Negatives Overexposed

(with apologies to Coleridge)

These pieces
of curated atomisation

these negatives
weakly overexposed

this marketplace
of transactional ennui

*water water everywhere*
*nor any drop to drink.*

## Dating as slush pile

Teetering stacks
of dismissed entreaties
crossing all genres
erotic fan fiction
romantic corn
pseudo psychological

(non) thrillers
misery memoirs
fantasy delusions
opening lines
of bathos and vacuity
narrative thinness

sodden dialogue
typos clichés repetitions
portraits rough-hewn
by an unfocussed eye
sorry boys:
no happy ending.

# To date an Asian woman

Not a lotus flower
in fragrant docility
an exotic bloom silk petal

black-curtain hair you can part
fingers in origami mode
creasing along the line

the hope of shaping a creature
who can bend over
backwards

learn my name
I'm not a mass of continents
a chopstick dish

to be poked
swallow a yellow fever pill,
no badge

for cultural appreciation
if you were to cross my border
and enter.

# Café au lait

So

where

are

you

*really*

from?

No answer<br>
                    so

                         I<br>
                               moved<br>
                                           closer

She was a black head

& those lips?

puffy pillow

glossy sheen

a smear in waiting

I could see she hailed

from some sweltering hell-hole

but maybe also

a splash of milk in there:

café au lait

I want to dip my spoon in

small but a tight little unit

you know?

Kawaii cute

China fragile

bamboo supple

but still she stares

coal-eyed inscrutable.

# Speed dating

Seven minutes
times twelve

swatch of skin tones
heads egg-polished

geeky-combed
smart-casual spritzed

clowns at a fun fair
Q&As popping out

everyone trying
to score

a prize in
this unlucky dip

a false economy
of numbers aligning

I walk out to an
empty clink.

# Agape

Eleven years faithful
these watchful walls
wifeandmother pin

tagged sharp
on breast
do not, do not look

you are
fenced in
now the gate is agape

a parade of passers-by
touting wares for rent
who to choose

this smile that profile
these gimmicks
and guiles

a travelling circus
of mirrors
and muscles:

Become ringleader
whip them in line.

# Things that are better than dating*

That high rise orange in the sky
marbled cat eyes in squints of sleep
a tri-coloured leaf downfoot
long daisy chain of friends
buttery crumbs with roasted beans
book flights sans passport & bags
wavelets of bubbled water
spoonfuls of feijoas sweetly tart
fountain pen swirls on virgin paper
this ermine cloak of self-worth.

* everything

# 'Something changed'

after Pulp

Whorls
of a fingerprint
interstices
of a snowflake
this singular form

whispered
into being
wefts crisscrossed
fine fabric spun
magicked from fairy dust

you:
baptised with tears
half real
half spirit
my Pygmalion dreaming

I want
a splinter
in the road
fish dropping
from the sky

I want
a carpet
of golden locusts
a miracle of
happenstance.

# 5 stars

I have taken apart many
unstitched pages
shone torches on stage
ripped celluloid reels
shower-praise and lambasted
as critic

Yet until you came along
and *wrote* on me
so carefully
I never knew the shiver
of technique
and pacing
and control
could undo me.

# Temperature

Even the sky was running a fever
and was flannel-cooled
when you came round
two hours before the new day

newly shorn cut close to your neck
my fingers
could wave through
what remained

the conversation roamed
and watered
with lukewarm tea
we took each other's measure:

what we produced
these last breakneck weeks
the creative tyrant that yoked
and unmade you

later you carried me over
we lay in twist
your lapis eyes
three-quarters shut

I knelt on the bed
coiled to a question mark
and you
you promised and left.

# Verb

You came at me
knife and fork in your eyes

I was curled like a comma
but there were no pauses

between us
no space at all

your column frame hard
your weight on top

your height stretched out
for me to scrape against

you made words
I was all sound

you in fast motion
a blur a slickness

a verb on rapid repeat.

# Two hours after two months

Pockets in the night
releasing you
postcodes apart

the beacon trail
of red tail-lights
dotted to me

days later
replay
not the urgency

but the slowness
my head bowed
in that nest

shoulder and neck
the room unseasonably
warm.

# Vertigo

Bare-limbed and straight-backed
we braced against the rising vowels

three times now I am only just
learning the language of your bones

the curve of your spine
as it grooves into me

not knowing this was the last
time our own Morse code

would be exchanged and interpreted
tiny vibrationsshudder

I need more than skin and surface talk
I am in too deep already

sunk in these pillows pulsing in time
weighted with urgency and air.

## Carpe Noctem

She wears black to defer to darkness

She wears black to absorb the stars

so she can glitter up within

She wears black so moonlight can bounce down her hair

and keep sliding

She wears black because night adores mischief

and she is awake.

## Grim(m)

What even are you?
a folklore creature
that shrivels
when the winter sun blinds
your breath stilled
by the chill
of appraising me
without night hiding us tight
a saviour protecting you
from expectations
in the whiteness of day

why can we not exist
outside these walls?
this holding pattern
of greeting and warming
in artificial time
only to wrench apart
before sunrise
you become shadow
and my head bows
too heavy for the stem that holds it.

# Metronome

Do you think I am that cocktail:
The Bloody Paloma
*delicate yet a little dangerous*
the fresh lime that tiny umbrella
a sprig of garnish on your day's end?

this metronome that beats fast
then suspends as your footsteps fade?

do I exist if not for your pleasure
a package blithely unpicked
and when you go that rustle
in your wake and then silence
your mind drinking elsewhere.

## Solid White Lines

Sorry, you said

I'm a simple man

and I thought, indeed:

middle of the road

baby blue eyes never askance

you are safe you won't swerve

& glance edgewise

all the difference I have

is not worth taking

an unmarked path

these loosened stones &

grit in the air

will just blind you

& zig-zag your map

all you want is a life

of solid white lines.

# Bello

That black leather jacket
soft skin a-drape
your torso an a(r)mour plating
a scripture of musculature
I am encouraged to read

it takes but an hour
like those *Choose*
*Your Own Adventure* books:
different endings but each
a little death.

# Words

Through a camera lens
across stage boards
dancing over pages
they hurtle through space

an invisible bridge
the stories that knit
mend the dissonance
between artifice and reality

from lower to uppercase
we speak of little and big
determinism and fate
the weight of our days

accounted
but now, here with me
the pause button pressed
you've stopped.

## Dusk

Serendipity
fate's merciful handmaiden
and here we are
Degraves Street
this Mecca to caffeine
black-on-black uniform
specials chalked
heat-emitting pillars
murmurings and clink

our conversation
a stream devoid of pebbles
our faces contoured
by tea-light candles
Van Gogh brushstrokes
flashes of colour
the blond of your hair
the red of my lips
the green of beginnings.

## Woken

There you are
for too long
a superior spectre
translucence I could see
right through
hovering on the trim
of dreams

there you are
coloured to the edges
flooding the empty
those dark-eyed touches
halting my breath
the gentlest of whispers:
I am here.

# Spring

The train was running late
stalactites in the bloodstream
wind cutting through marrow
a woebegone statue
snap sapped

but the thought of you
pushes blush to the surface
pinkness licking back the grey
a crawl of feeling
to the deadened

see the blossoms are out
tiny white velvet
catching the sunrise
the soft scent of new
airborne already.

# Koi

A somersaulting fish
in the ribcage
when I see you turn the corner
briny and reddish-gold

thrashing
it flips high
wanting to vault
to reach you

pearlescent scales
shedding disc by
half moon disc.

## Pillow Book

Don't dilettante
like you have a paper cut
we are a chapter over

in the pages
I want us to spill
crumbs and morning after

coffee as we lie
with buttermilk sun
sneaking between shutters

there is a library
to be collected
of what is yet unwritten

let's start with your spine
I want to read History
then Art

followed by the fiction
in your eyes
after which those fingers

can flip all the way through
find the right spot
bookmark me.

## Half-wink

You had me
when I saw that semicolon
gentle half-wink
a pause, but then that finger curl

cheekiness and intent
anyone can place a comma,
a little trip, a crease in the smooth
but that mark right there

made me stumble
a levelling    a balance
speaks of the measure of us
you had me; you really did.

## Interrobang

That eyebrow raise
and then a starter
pistol as you jump

towards me a blur
in force so quick
the alarm clock rattles

beside us and beads
of water drip from
your brow into

my waiting mouth
there is salt and salt
to swallow dry.

## Sphinx

I fear
if touched
you would mirage
melt into sand

not for this firmament
a scaffolding
for my desires
you would drop

a sprinkle of dust
held by hope
and torched by too bright
a flame I held

for you I must
soft patter back
to safety
to distance

wait in shade
til your sun
revolves across
and falls on me.

# Fallen

The gods are playing with me
a chorus-smirk from the wings
push forth this bespoke man

stretched out unseen pins
the cut unruched and silky
mannequin polished

from end to end
a litany he duly preached
to words the solid weight of them

the workshipful religion
and for me a fellow believer
he was gold dust and angel.

# Negative space

We were looking the same way
a gravitational pull
and in that glance
planets collided and reformed

twin forces lit through dark matter
but the stars
the stars aligned not
distracted for a beat

a heavenly body in your path
and you spun away
off-course on another axis
and left me spinning.

# Triple word score

A-I-R-I-L-Y

that word you put down

a triple score that won

over me what else could I do

in defeat but bestow a kiss

W-I-L-L-I-N-G-L-Y

that hand that led you over

to the bed already crumpled

in wait of more play:

Twister without a spinner

H-E-S-I-T-A-N-T-L-Y

cues that were to be read

in semi-darkness but I can't see

the widening of your pupils

when touch went there and there

B-R-A-Z-E-N-L-Y

guess and feather point anyway

alternate with firmer grip and

pause and change and move repeat

into atop over around under through.

a tangle of nouns and prepositions.

## Pace

Do you see me as delicious
lubricious
        when we met
        did it set
the course to auspicious?

our movements kinetic
balletic
        was it an honour
        such hard-won bonheur
your faith before? heretic

trickles of hours to taste
haste!
        seconds will fly
        stars evolving to die
foot off the pedal keep pace.

## Kismet

My stockings fishnet
your eyes so wet
this big love debt
all set:
kismet

your dear heart? not yet
rubbed out then stet
too soon first met
all set:
kismet

no mere toy or  pet
not me in your net
you sure won't get
all set:
kismet.

## Eclipse

Sun or moon
will you create
or reflect
heat
& light

will there be
lambent flicks
of wit:
such flutter
of moth wings

whispery
fingertips that
dance across me
& contour breast
like an eclipse

can you hold
the weight of
my skull in the
hollow of
your hand?

# Turn-off

The paths taken and forsaken
plots chosen or remaindered

these leaps of faith on edge
stumble back to dirt trail

you on one side
and me, my shoulder now angled

away the sharp collarbone
cuts into the misty glade

a soft crunch underfoot                                        a
glance behind then quiet.

## Distance

Here and there
is a long way
even those swallows
on your collarbone

would struggle
to ride the wind:
how can you to me
stay the distance?

but from sun fall to rise
though mirror doubled
we came as one,
breaths in tandem

ragged and sweaty
soft-eyed sly-tongued:
a solid bridging
trust on even scaffolds

that night was grasped
trapped hard
in amber and
glittering aspic.

# Syntax

The keening of us
the spaces between
a kerning too distant
your clauses conditional
dashes sprinting away
I didn't want to be modified
& left dangling
but you trailed into ellipsis
and left me falling through gaps.

# Legato

It was as though you set it up
those bursts of neon
temporary stars
that glorified the sky

plumes of syncopated flashes
exploding over rooftops
but here on the 22nd floor
spirographs are at bay

there's only muted booms
and in my ear the soft rasp
of you and in my eyes
penumbra and half tones

and through your touch a rhythm
adagio to coda to what started earlier
in the car against the street wall
and when you took my hand.

# Saltwater

When the oyster is pearled open
when the sky is conch blushed
when waves of moontide hum in your ear

I need you to breathe me back to life
cool hand on the brow
to jumpstart what had arrested

splay your fingers across the breastbone
a pressure a rise a flickering
and stay there a beat then two

I need you to open my eyes
lashes stiff with saltwater
to see footprints washed out in your wake.

# Evanescence

Because of you
this star turned itself off
drew the black over
its lustre to dim
retreated to base
drifted

to other corners
a month of low wattage
in wane and splutter
I once thought we could
split open the horizon
to create a new world.

# Harvest Moon

Please
arise and look about
rub the dregs from your eyes
this cold tea day is ending

can you not see
the moon,
this balloon
tethered on string?

dutiful, round-faced
a slow bounce
witness and provocateur
it waits

how many more cycles
phases sliced then fulsome
out of tippy-toe reach
before you find me?

# Invisible Ink

A flare of textual chemistry
& you are perched on the bed
guitar in hand
my taste in your mouth

smooth-skinned
are you waiting for indents
for chords unstrung
reason for song?

upon you invisible ink
yet to be marked
by my heart's pen
there is cat wariness

from me and unable to see
the greenness of your eyes
a wait for clarity of sun
a loosening of intent.

## Meridian

Let's just meet
in the middle
from worlds
unfathomable
you and me

both blown off compass
miles from shore
no buoy or anchor
let's just taste the sea

what's true north
or wrong-hearted
is washed away
let's just float free

no divide between skin
so let's join up
reach out
silken the waves
just you and me.

# Dangerous Curves Ahead

1.
One passion(fruit) cocktail down
my pulse disrupted
a giggle-grasp onto you
across the slick wet tarmac

Too night to see your eyes
the irises change
against the light
so you say and I wonder

of your constancy: do you hold
in slippery weather?

2.
The bath: you're an armchair
straight-backed warm and hard
I nestle against the water
my seaweed hair a lazy throw over

3.
I'm a siren in red and black
you're sculptured rock
teeth flashing at the warning:
dangerous curves ahead.

# Memento Mori

This is you moving in me
these are your eyes
weighing me down

This is the mirror of our souls
these are the mouths
soft and sibilant

This is the darkness closing in
these are the moments
of quiet remembrance

This is the chase and the conquest
these are the fruits
to be savoured slow

This is your skull warm on touch
these are the hearts
beating for now.

# Postmodernism

Weary of triptych classicism:

genesis, hubris, nemesis

I pray for postmodern flux

uncertain start

stretch to infinity

your deconstruction

my reinvention

to exist in that liminal

lick of blue flamed kerosene sky

before it burns into day.

# Ligature

The world is colonised by meaning

even the dot above the i

has been lassoed – a tittle

but what you are to me

not yet sweet-talked and caged

undefined the bonds are slack

you can take yourself for a walk

sans souci sans serif

bolden without my strokes

trailing your every turn

you & me? a brand new font

soft-bellied hard-edged

characters of looping swashes

accentuated glyphs

a ligature in the making.

# Turbulence

## ‘In the Mood for Love’

after Bryan Ferry

The tram stutters
she falls into him
his chin on her crown
a jut that steadies
her face angled
a peck on feathered cheek
a responding coo
his overcoat a winged embrace

another two loiter
slumming it
broken glass
and graffiti screams
sleek unlined skin
beneath distressed denim
camera phone aloft
behold the millennial moue

There, another pair
wispy hair flying
a swirl of slate wind
he pushes through first
her hand in his palm
she one beat behind
in footsteps
cleared of debris

they are everywhere
these lovers
I watch
a trespasser
I watch
through triple-glazed glass
with a cynic's head
a poet's heart.

# In memoriam

for Jeff

I keep seeing you
your dimply grins
hand on my lower back
to centre me
I am off-kilter
a childish storm cloud
of petulance brimming
you just laugh
steer me aslant
letting in newly washed air

you coax me onto your bike
the fishbowl wedged tight
I cannot talk
but my arms round your waist
the thrill of corners
cut fast
cars left blinking behind
eyes closed
breath stilled
I trust.

# Pegasus

for Jeff

It's been twelve months
since I heard
your heart
it stopped

the last time I saw you
spent in sheets
I kissed adieu
left that city room

Pegasus Hotel
such aptness
destroys me even now
my white-winged love

for such faithful service
on his last day of life
Pegasus flew
with the stars

it's been twelve months
since I heard
your heart
it stopped.

# Moving pictures

for Jo

To the number of times we've lolled
sated by door-deliveries
sweets table-topped scattered
sugared pops to lift
through the drag of night
to the quantity of tears
the equivalence of junk food
to the tales of junk men
who dared to treat *us* as throwaways
from 80s cult to Austen prim
to the real drama
our harried words so streaming rushed
a waterfall of confusion
we tried to sip in cup-size portions
to my beloved friend
to these last few years
your kindness against the blows
to such ministrations
now you distantly away
and I think of us often
to whispering traffic
to confidence huddles
framed and foreshortened
by the strolling river
to lolly-coloured shipping containers
to twinkling towers rising to the sky.

## Vale Anthony Bourdain

Life is for the eating the belching the saliva spits the scraping of tiny
plastic stools on chaotic rubbish strewn streets horns in concert with
the clacking of chopsticks on cracked bowls the gelatinous noodle
broth slurps the eye dripping nose reddened spicy mistakes.

Life is not for making reservations but for turning up and hoping a
table's free in the smack of busy parts unknown of roads unwashed
of being lost and knotted in a whirligig trusting there's a way out
of seeking succor of being touched by random hearts and letting
yourself be singed by that flame.

# Vale Eurydice

Tenderstruck
there are flickers
on strikes of
artificial light
wan in the squall
warmth in congregation
an open plain
a shedding of flowers
prostrate shaking
saying your name
means wide justice
but now once again
shadows will be jumped
twig break a warning
the sky on the crack
of becoming a bruise.

# Beautiful mess

Galaxies are drifting
and you, like the cosmos

are a beautiful mess
this orbital debris

of floating space junk
you've lost your way

tripping constellations
stardust in your eyes

want also means lack
a hole in time

you try to fill
with these passing rocks

fluorescent-shelled
that crumple after touch

this is the only universe
to spin in

I say hitch that asteroid ride
climb the altitudes

where your breath is thin
and your head dizzy

you'll get there
the sun warming your back.

## Skylight

That pressure turns into diamonds
sharp cut angles
screaming when forged
weight pushed from all sides
dirt falling in my mouth
this airlessness a gift
I did not know until now
that darkness carries a candle.

# Together: After Escher

For everything to fall into place
those tessellated planes
interlocked to infinity

upwards or downwards
landscape stretched and
your refracted reflection

in that glass dome with domestic
order behind the serene geometry
of your eyes in direct stare

black traverse into white
fish jump-flying into birds
lizards eating their own tails

this other dimension a new time
a new space where the impossible
is stark: depth in the shallow.

## Birthday

As tender is the day
and baleful is the night

offer the past
an eviction notice

take, take what you can
a swag of trinkets

to honour and bless
a keepsake of goodness:

an arrow can only be shot
by pulling it backwards

then it can launch
into thistle or moss

it matters not
there is now distance.

# Insert eye roll emoji (Why people don't read modern poetry)

Maybe because

line drops and see here
these tics

of gratuitous style insert some random

Latinate *bon mots* so the uncouths
will stumble and then continue
kickkkking

when they are down and fogged up
With a [ ] pair of [ ] because it's [ ] [ ]

What about compoundnounsthatrunlike this
Something here about the glory of native bush even tho
you have never been beyond zone 3 on PT

Add doleful '...' Beckettian misery here
(Phew, your 20th century Lit Minor was not a waste!)

So winning so woke you never even zzz

Rhymes r for babies, you gotta put your ass - on - ance

Continue to fill up the page just

Break it up

## DISRUPTING THE DOMINANT PARADIGM IS DOPE

More is Less is Less is More

Now work in a simile like a metaphor
boa constricting
a riddle

@&%%# looks good doesn't it?

## History disrupted

The Singer machine

my mother's hands

the bobbin the pedal

frayed threads on denim

her eyes tiny buttons

unseeing beyond

metres and metres

just to sew me

a clean life of ink and

cloistered hallways

where dead white males

ghost through all ages:

Banquo's looking glass

a modern ermine trail

of blue-tinged pale kings

to the last of days...

lest you forget we own this land

our father his father and his

before were here already

carved and divided

so if you want a patch

to seed your hopes

better prick your thumbs woman

back to the needle the whirr

only from your blood

dusk-hollowed

husk-nourished

your child will fatten

outgrow this box

stealth across barriers

purloin sceptres

and disrupt history.

# Cusp

for Ava

You are twelve
eye level with me
though feet have stretched ahead
just as well; you can't fit my shoes
you need to bright away from my shadow
chalkmark your life map
and jump small or big

a dozen years concertinaed
and it's come to this:
colt gait across the stage
resolute half-frown
crinkling over the soft-smooth
in your hands a document:
the end and the beginning

a new school ahead
crooked paths that'll mark
and forge and make you
a longer leash from me
invisible and slack:
from heart to heart
beats behind I'll always follow.

# Turbulence

Mourning morning
a sky of dirty sheets
aloft on a green wave
this ladybird on a leaf
rides the gutters
a pinprick
of red

a fat drop splashes
she flies into dry
seeing her tiny wings
I defy the clouds
and curl
and brace
into the day.

# Acknowledgements

"Sunflower" has been published online in *Mascara Literary Review.*

"Pestle", "Lodestar: To Ava", "See-Saw", "Words", "Dusk" and "Insert eye roll emoji" have been been published online in *Eureka Street.*

"Beautiful Mess" and "Vertigo" have been published in *Gargouille* literary journal.

"Interrobang" and "Pillow Book" have been published online in *Lor* journal.

"Tu me manques", "Despondentrage", "Koi" and "Triple Word Score" have been published online in *Djed Press.*

"Verb" has been published online in *Meniscus.*

"Dating as Slush Pile" has been published online in *Foam:e*

"Surface", "Double bind" and "Mosaic" have been published in *Myriad* Magazine.

"In the Mood for Love" (After Bryan Ferry), "Astor" and "Something Changed" (After Pulp) have been published online in *Stereo Stories*.

"Perspective" has been published in the Dec 2018/Jan 2019 edition of *Writers Victoria* newsletter.

"To Date an Asian Woman" has been published in *Australian Poetry Anthology Volume 7, 2019.*

"Half-Wink" has been published in *Antithesis.*

"Centrifugal Forces" has been published in the anthology, *We are Here (2019).*

Thank you to the Wheeler Centre for granting me a Hot Desk Fellowship and the Readings Foundation for providing the accompanying stipend for work on *Turbulence*. Also to Penguin Random House for shortlisting the manuscript in their Write it Fellowship program.

Thank you to everyone who has read and provided feedback to earlier drafts of these poems; your sustained support has enabled me to steer *Turbulence* into calmer waters.

In particular, I remain deeply indebted to Terri-ann White and her team at the University of Western Australia Publishing, to my long-suffering family, as well as to the following friends and cheerleaders:

Donna Ward, Jordie Albiston, Kevin Brophy, Michelle Cahill, Maxine Beneba Clarke, Melanie Cheng, Georgia Gowing, Jenny Thompson, David Nichols, Joanne Vizzari, Anna Solding, Rosa Papasergi, Jackie Tang, Raphaelle Race, Susan Wyndham, Angela Savage, Susan Johnson, Miranda Tay, Dash Maiorova, Rahne Widarsito, Michael Dollin, Nicolette Vaszolyi, Kent MacCarter, Emma Hegarty, Vicki Renner, Lee Kofman, James Tierney, Angela Smith, Chris Phillips, Paul Dalgarno, Kate Mulqueen, Louise Correcha, Colin Donald, Nick Gadd, Rochelle Siemienowicz, Meg Mundell, Chris Boyd, S.A.Jones, Matt Millis, Aaron Walton, Matthew Hardy and Luke Pirois.

Darling Ava –
one day you'll understand.